A Tale of
Two Continents

Jetting Across the Globe to Have a Baby

Arnelle Kendall

iUniverse, Inc.
Bloomington

A Tale of Two Continents
Jetting Across the Globe to Have a Baby

iUniverse books may be ordered through booksellers or by contacting:

iUniverse
1663 Liberty Drive
Bloomington, IN 47403
www.iuniverse.com
1-800-Authors (1-800-288-4677)

ISBN: 978-1-4502-6253-8 (pbk)
ISBN: 978-1-4502-6254-5 (cloth)
ISBN: 978-1-4502-6252-1 (ebk)

Printed in the United States of America

iUniverse rev. date: 2/3/11

To Heather, Ivor, and Shaelah,
the joy of my life.

Contents

Preface

In the last decade or so, increasing numbers of women have been opting for in vitro fertilization as a method of having a baby when no special partner was in their lives and time was running out. I fit squarely into that category.

At the same time, my experience with giving birth in vitro was different—even unique. The path I followed to have my precious daughter, Shaelah, led me through an ordeal that surely was unprecedented.

The enormous difficulties I faced were largely a result of the unusual process of selecting a donor that I originated. I did not want to simply accept the sperm of an anonymous donor at a sperm bank. Instead, I asked friends in my native South Africa to donate sperm, and no one, including myself, would know whose was chosen. Thus my eggs would be fertilized by the sperm of a man with good genes and a good background, and one whom I much respected.

But little did I know about the complications and crushing disappointments that would ensue in my trips to and from

Johannesburg, nor the pain I would endure because of a precancerous condition.

I hope this book inspires other women who are left with no other alternative for giving birth to seriously consider in vitro fertilization as a means of realizing their dreams. Compared to my ordeal, the average in vitro experience should be a cakewalk.

Then, too, I want this book to show Shaelah, when she is older, just how special she is.

Chapter 1

Saying Goodbye

$\mathcal{A}$ youngster who not long ago was on all fours is coaxing my old piano, an upright, out of retirement. The irony is striking, even if the harmony is muddled.

The little one is my daughter. She's been giving the Hoffman keyboard quite a workout since graduating from the crawling level to the curiosity stage.

That piano, situated in the living room of my home in Boca Raton, Florida, has come a long way, baby—and the baby, now a toddler, has come just as far. Both the keyboard and my precious little daughter paradoxically symbolize a break from, and connection with, the past.

Not that it was a bad past. To convert literal distance into the metaphorical: far from it. I was born Dec. 19, 1962, in the Republic of South Africa. Bordered by the Atlantic Ocean on the west and the Indian Ocean on the east, it is the southernmost country on the continent. South Africa is blessed with the most pleasant climate imaginable and a wonderfully variegated landscape that ranges from grassland to lush subtropical to mountainous. Leaving it was enormously difficult—likely the hardest thing I've ever done, for two reasons.

First was a fear of the unknown that loomed on the other side of the world. It was akin to facing death. That prospect was perhaps mitigated by a previous encounter I'd had with the real Great Beyond as a young woman (more on that later). Even more emotionally wrenching—the part that broke my heart—was saying goodbye to my dear friends and the homeland that I loved.

Nonetheless, there were issues that drove home the realization I could no longer stay. My vision of a bright future in America proved prescient, because that move gave me a new lease on life. Actually, forget the lease. It gave me a new life—literally. Her name is Shaelah.

The path to her birth was strewn with more obstacles than a mountain road after an avalanche. That was partly because, in the interest of having the baby, I never completely severed the umbilical cord linking me with my beloved South Africa. Yet, despite the anguishing complications caused by that lingering connection, it turned out for the best. Shaelah's debut on planet Earth is a tale of two continents. She has roots in both, and was a world traveler before she was even born.

I made the decision to move to America in 1997. On August 9 of that year, my two best friends, Margit Pilz and Tommy Schmidt, both of whom I'd worked with many years in the travel industry, picked me up and drove me to Johannesburg International Airport. On the way, I cried my eyes out, because I never had imagined that I'd live anywhere else. I felt as though my world were coming to an end. It was like a nightmare in which I was outside my body.

I boarded a flight for Miami, and it's a good thing I didn't make the trip on an ocean liner, because my tears would have sunk it. Okay, that's a bit of a stretch. But I must have used up half the plane's supply of Kleenex. I was crying so much that the crew gave me tea bags for my eyes. From Miami, I drove to Boca Raton to join my mother, who had settled in the upscale South Florida city after leaving Johannesburg three years earlier. She, too, had spent all of her life there.

Chapter 2

In The Spotlight

*J*ohannesburg is a bustling, cosmopolitan city the size of, say, San Francisco, or Memphis. Like South Africa in general, it is socially progressive, ethnically diverse and culturally vibrant. The family I grew up in took full advantage of that culture.

I was raised by my mother, Heather, and my maternal grandparents, Jack and Phyllis Smith, and had a wonderful childhood. My mother and father divorced when I was eighteen months old, at a time when it was unheard of in South Africa to get divorced. That willingness to flout convention took a lot of courage for her. I think she passed that independent streak on to me, because in having my baby, I also chose an unorthodox route.

Jack and Phyllis cared for me while my mother worked as an accountant. We had a great life together. The whole family was so vibrant. We weren't poor, but we weren't rich. My mother cherishes the memories, as do I, and loves to tell about one of her fondest:

"My father became Arnelle's father figure. She was crazy about him, and every night she used to stand on the apartment balcony waiting for him to come home from work. But she was too short to see over the balcony, so she would stand on a little doll stool and lean on the balcony. As soon as he would pull up, she would scream, 'Jackie boy! What did you bring me?' And he loved it. All the neighbors loved it, too. Because she was this little thing, about three years old."

Among my most precious memories as a little girl were the Saturdays when my mother and her mother's side of the family would go to the horse races. They were all involved in horseracing—as breeders, jockeys and trainers. My uncle and aunt owned stables, and they would look after me as they tended the horses and I walked around the stables with them, until my mother would pick me up at the end of the day. So I was brought up in this horseracing fraternity, and yet I never learned to ride. It's hard to believe.

My grandfather was a skilled craftsman and had a flair for mathematics. My grandmother was quite a good amateur singer and entertainer, and had a passion for the arts and theater. My mother was steeped in dance. They passed those genes onto me, and I used them to forge an early, professional career on the stage and as a model. I learned a lot from all three of them.

My aspiration early on was to dance. My mother had me dancing when I was three. I started in ballet, then went on to American jazz, and eventually became schooled in tap and Spanish—flamenco. At age 13, I turned professional in dancing. But I was also active in the theater department at my school, winning lots of acting and singing awards, and I decided this was the way to go—to make a career in the theater.

That beautiful walnut piano, probably about seventy years old, in my home played a key (pun unintended) role in the development of my talents. It belonged to my grandparents, and my grandmother left it to me when she died of Alzheimer's disease. She would accompany me on it when I sang and danced in preparation for auditions to perform in shows. After a full day of school, I would perform in the shows at night. I was in my early teens, and lied about my age to get the jobs because South African law forbade children from working before age seventeen. My earliest show-biz experience was working in the Circus Osler, a children's circus.

Probably the highlight of those wonderful early-teen times when I strutted and fretted my hour upon the stage was my involvement in a British musical called *The Boyfriend*, a throwback to the 1920s flapper era of boy-meets-girl musicals. It was written in the 1950s and last performed in England by the Oxford Operatic Society in 1980. It turned out to be a harbinger of the kind of life I would later yearn for, but never realize. One song was particularly telling: *It's Never*

Too Late to Fall in Love. I played Maisie, one of the girls—
an inveterate teaser—in the Madame Dubonnet finishing
school. It turned out to be a fitting role for me, because it
presaged my matriculation in a real finishing school a couple
of years later. The show was chock-full of songs popular in
the Roaring Twenties, along with scintillating choreography,
including some strictly acrobatic dance maneuvers that I
executed as Maisie.

It was a great show and received great reviews, and I
was offered a bursary, or scholarship, to study at Oxford
University in London. But I couldn't accept it because I had
lied about my age. You had to be sixteen, and I was only
fourteen.

While I was singing and dancing to the downbeat, my
dad was being a classic deadbeat. He paid no child support.
My mother paid for everything—my dance lessons, ballet
shoes, Spanish dance shoes, tap shoes—the whole works.
Later on, as I progressed, I paid for my own dance lessons
and studied several years in the school of Martha Graham,
who was famous in South Africa as well as America. But in
the meantime, my dad had abandoned me, never coming to
visit, or even acknowledging my birthdays or contacting me
on holidays. My mother remembers those years well, so I'll
let her do the talking here:

"When Arnelle was about fourteen, she was in all the
newspapers because of the shows she performed in. Her

father no doubt was reading all of these glowing things written about her, so he phoned up. 'I'm calling to see how my baby is,' he said. And I said, 'There are no babies here.' And that was it. We never heard from him again."

So I think it was out of a desire to atone for her son's shortcomings that my paternal grandmother asked me to come and live with her in Australia when I was sixteen so she could put me through finishing school. I enrolled in the June Dally Watkins School of Modeling in Sydney, and studied modeling, fashion, continuity (learning to speak on television), elocution, makeup, etiquette, and deportment. You learned how to be lady.

As time wore on, it became increasingly difficult for my family members and me to be apart from each other. Fax machines and the Internet with its e-mail were still in the pioneering stages, so communicating was by phone, which was awfully expensive, or telex. My mother and I would talk on the phone and she would cry, telling me how much she and my grandparents missed me. And I was missing them, too. Remember *The Brady Bunch*? We were The Boo Hoo Bunch—not much like the TV family, but a bit unconventional, nonetheless. So, after a year in Australia, I returned to my home in Johannesburg.

I joined a modeling agency called Penny Bowden Elite, which was part of the Johnny Casablancas Modeling and Career Centers, an international agency that was based in the United States and remains very much alive and thriving. I continued my studies there and was recruited for jobs in modeling and television commercials, and for dancing parts in shows. The opportunities were bountiful, and I took full advantage of them, covering the gamut of roles embraced by that field. As time went on and I became increasingly independent, my mother began to think about remarrying. She had decided to wait until I was twenty-one to do so because she wanted to see me grown up and completely able to make my way on my own. And I wanted my mom to have a happy life. As a little girl, I would go to bed every night and pray, "Dear God, let my mother meet somebody nice. I want my mother to be happy." After I turned twenty-one, my prayers were answered as she carried out her plan and married Ivor Marsden, the national accountant for a big supermarket chain in South Africa. So my mother changed her moniker again, becoming Heather Marsden in a family with more names than a character in a Russian novel. She went from Smith to Ossendryver to Marsden, and I, without even marrying, went from Arnelle Ossendryver to Arnelle Kendall Ossendryver. How did the Kendall come about? My grandmother had decided that Ossendryver, a Dutch-Jewish name, was too long and cumbersome for a person in show business, and gave me a middle name, Kendall, after English actress Kay Kendall, who had herself changed her real name of McCarthy to that of her maternal grandmother.

I use Ossendryver for legal purposes, but people know me as Kendall.

The life of performing and modeling that I was leading during those teenage years and into my early twenties was strenuous, with hectic schedules and intense pressures, but the work was sporadic. Sometimes I was so busy that I hardly had time to eat and sleep. Nonetheless, I found it highly rewarding, although there were periods of inactivity, which left one feeling less than secure financially. Show biz is tough, and unless you're a big star, you have to supplement your career with other kinds of work in order to make ends meet. So I enrolled in college courses in public relations and marketing, while working in sales and marketing for a small hotel group during the day. It all worked okay for several years—until, when I was twenty-three, it all came apart.

Chapter 3

Heading Off Death

*I*t was the start of the Easter weekend and I was in Johannesburg, giving a presentation about the hotel group to a large assemblage of executive secretaries, when I felt a burst in my brain. It felt like pins and needles in my left side and in my arm. And all at once I felt this gush, and there were colors—green, blue, orange, yellow—around me. Some of the women told me later that they could see the blood had drained from my face and I was white as a ghost. In fact, I was closer to entering the spirit world than any of them realized at the time. I felt this bile forming in my mouth, and I was awfully nauseated. So I said, "Excuse me," and ran out of the room. But after a few minutes I felt better, and returned. I apologized to the group of women and carried on with the lecture. But afterward I felt sick again, so I quickly went to see a doctor.

He said, "You know, you're under a lot of stress, and it's probably a bad migraine headache." And I told him, "Well, I may be under stress, but I handle all these different stresses. I thrive under stress."

That was on a Thursday. The following day was Good Friday of Easter weekend, and I had planned to have some people over for brunch at my mother's house, where I was staying with my grandparents and their dogs while my mother and stepfather were in Australia, opening a big supermarket. My cousin Darene came first, and I told her I felt really ill. She insisted on taking me to see the doctor, who checked me out and again said nothing was wrong—that I must have had a migraine. From there we went to the hospital, where an X-ray of my head was taken, and nothing was found. I guess my head was empty—like that of baseball legend Dizzy Dean, who, after having X-rays for possible trauma from getting beaned with a ball, told reporters, "They X-rayed my head and found nothing." So I went home and made brunch for all these people, dragging my leg from kitchen to dining room.

The next night, Saturday, I had a date and was so excited. But it was the worst, because the guy must have thought I was out of it. My foot was dragging, and I could hardly focus on him. I had a drink of soda water and lime juice, but could hardly hold the glass. The guy probably wondered, "What is she on?" All day Sunday, I lay in bed, ill. My grandfather, Jack Smith, applied heat to my left side, where I was feeling pins and needles. The next day was Easter Monday, a religious holiday in South Africa, but I planned to go to my office in the city and work. I got in my car, but climbed back out because my vision was so bad. So my uncle, Courtney, took me to see ophthalmologist Jonathan Levine, who took one look and said, "There's something not right. It's more than the eyes." He phoned Dr. Les Cohen, a neurologist, who booked me straight into the hospital and took a brain scan and did a spinal tap. I remember negotiating with him: "If you don't hurt me, you can have two nights at the Inyati safari lodge." And it wasn't bad, so I kept my word. When the results came back, he said, "We are seeing something behind the optic nerve, and it looks like a tumor, and it's not good. It's not good. It's in a very dangerous part of the brain."

My Aunt Olivia returned on the Blue Train from a trip to Capetown and came to the hospital. I told her, "Don't tell my mom, because I don't want her to panic." But after talking to Dr. Cohen, she phoned my mother in Australia and told her she needed to come back at once. My mother flew home, and by then my condition worsened, so I was transferred to another hospital for more tests, including an angiogram. Something went wrong with the procedure and I ended up in the intensive care unit for a few days. Finally, the diagnosis was a tumor. Further, I was bleeding in the brain. We all met, and the doctors said surgery would be necessary. Otherwise, I would live only three weeks because the tumor was growing rapidly. And I'm my mother's only child, and she was devastated. She said, "No, I want another opinion."

I'll let her tell it:

"They said the tumor was growing daily. And I asked what the chances were if we did surgery. They said she could be permanently blind and she could be left crippled down her left side. And I said, 'Will she *need* a brain if she can't see, she can't walk? What are you actually predicting as the outcome of this?' I told them I was going to get other opinions. I ended up with nine doctors, because I used to work in the medical profession. And one of them told me he didn't think it was a tumor. He thought it was an aneurysm."

That's pretty much the way it happened. After the tests were done and I left the hospital, however, the ophthalmologist was given the results and agreed with the doctors at the hospital that it looked like a tumor. I said to my mother, "I refuse to believe it. I refuse to believe it. I won't believe that I have a tumor." You know, when you have that, your chances of surviving are not good. I was living on my own at the time, and I moved in with my mother. As she said, we started seeking help from other doctors. And one neurosurgeon told us, "Let's do a brain biopsy." He said that the cutting instrument entering my brain might sever all of my nerves down the left side, and I would be paralyzed. But that price would be worth paying, he said, because it would enable the doctors to know what was wrong.

Mom: "I said, 'No.' And he said to me, 'You have no right to give her a death sentence. She's over 21, and she can say what's to be done, not you.' And he went on and on and on. We left, and he began calling me at home. And I prayed, 'Please God. This man is driving me mad, and I'm putting this in your hands.' But he finally persuaded us that a biopsy was the only way to find out how to treat Arnelle, and she was admitted to the hospital and scheduled for surgery the next morning. I stayed in the hospital overnight with Arnelle. When morning came, the neurosurgeon walked into the room and said he had to postpone the surgery because the drill for entering the skull was broken. And I said, 'That's a message from God. We're out of here.'"

So we didn't do it. But I was in terrible condition. My left side was dragging, and I couldn't drive a car because I could hardly see.

After she remarried, my mother had begun breeding racehorses and racing them, and was planning a trip to the United States to consider purchasing horses at stables in the Lexington, Kentucky, area for breeding in South Africa. She decided that I should come along and stop in New York to get another doctor's opinion. A cousin of my mother's husband, Dr. Selwyn Supra, who was a professor of optometry at Rand Afrikaans University (RAU) in Johannesburg, had been monitoring my eyesight and made special glasses that enabled me to see peripherally. I saw him weekly for tests, and each time he said my eyesight had improved. He referred us to Dr. Raymond H. Coll, a top-ranked neurologist in New York City. He was from Johannesburg and received part of his medical training there. So, lugging a case with all of my brain CAT scans and angiograms, I joined my mother on a flight to America's city of cities. I can imagine what the reaction of an airport security checker today would be upon scanning my scans. "Is this a joke, lady? We only need to know what's *on* your body, not *in* your body—and certainly not in your head."

The support from my colleagues in the travel industry was wonderful. I had a surprise at the airport—an upgrade in my seat to first class.

We arrived in New York, the first visit there for either of us. We'd heard all about the Big Apple, and it didn't disappoint. Everything was so big. At the medical center, Dr. Coll ran tests and inspected the scans I'd brought. He said, "Normally, with what you've got, this kind of tumor, your memory would start to go. You would go totally blind. And one day you wouldn't wake up." Then, as if to make sure I'd gotten the point: "You'd be dead."

So Dr. Coll tested my memory and put me through all sorts of other trials to determine my levels of cognition and coordination, etcetera. Everything came back pretty good, so he took a series of large X-rays and had other experts at the center read them. Then he came back down the hall to the room where my mother and I were waiting, and uttered the sweetest words I've ever heard. "You know what? What those doctors in South Africa were seeing was a scar sitting on the optic nerve, caused by the bleeding." He said an aneurysm had formed and burst. "The blood formed a bubble and became a scar when it dried. It was like a scab. And they thought that was a tumor. But you obviously have peripheral vision."

The doctor said that it would be too dangerous to attempt removal of the scar, and I should just let it heal by itself. He told me not to lift anything heavy or swim underwater to avoid any pressure on the brain, and prescribed aspirin every day and a Scotch whisky now and then.

We returned to South Africa. My mother told me I needed to take an aerobics instructor's course and teach it because it would be good physical therapy and a less stressful way to earn a living. I took the course three times a week and spent hours practicing, but didn't pass it. I didn't enjoy aerobics.

Even though I'm a qualified dancing teacher. I couldn't believe it. But I refused to let this little setback damage my ego, figuring my cerebellum had suffered enough trauma. I would merely accept the reality that I was handicapped. Nonetheless, the course by itself helped me physically for the short time that it lasted. I started to move again. Everything began coming back—though I was still far from normal.

And what did Mom say about my recovery? The same thing she always says when we're faced with adversity: "You cannot keep the Smith girls down."

But I had to reduce my work load, and I couldn't maneuver around the stage or walk the runway, anyway, because my left side was still dragging. I suppose I could have done my own version of performing in drag. And my peripheral vision was limited, as well. I was offered the job of reservations manager for the Inyati Game Lodge, a few hours northeast of Johannesburg in the famed Sabi Sand Game Reserve, from which adventurers went on safaris and took photos of The Big Five of the African animal kingdom: elephants, lions, leopards, cheetahs, and buffalo. I accepted. It was not an easy decision, because I knew it meant the end of my performance career. I decided: You know what? I love the arts, I love the theater—but I need to move on. This job was just what the doctor ordered. I told myself, you don't need to be a big, fancy-schmancy executive. For what?

Because this experience really affected me. It very much changed my perspective. I went through a terrible death depression. I kept thinking: *What is it all about? What is life? Where are we going afterward? Is there a God, or isn't there?* And every Sunday was the worst time for me. I felt somewhat lonely, in a black hole. Actually, Sundays always have been bleak and dismal for me, with the weekend wrapping up and another work week about to begin. But during this period, the day became one of doom and gloom. Through self-analysis I finally was able to overcome those feelings.

I joined Inyati with no big ambitions. All I wanted to do was enjoy life, and not kill myself working. But Inyati was owned by a group of ten very well-to-do businessmen who knew nothing about the hotel business or travel industry. It wasn't long before they promoted me from reservations to managing the lodge. So, despite my hope of leading a more leisurely life, I was off and running again. The lodge was averaging only sixteen percent occupancy, and in eight months I had it operating at full capacity, in-season and out-of-season. I just built it up. My strength gradually returned to normal, as did my walking. I regained ninety percent of my eyesight. The damage was on my left side, and I fortunately was right-handed. My grandmother had always forced me to do things with my right hand, because anyone who frequently used the left hand was regarded as lacking in social graces in South Africa. So I quickly learned to write and do other things again, although I still can't carry very heavy objects. Concomitantly with the physical revitalization came a resurgence of my old drive to achieve, and I again became a workaholic.

In time I moved up the ladder to general manager for the whole company. I handled the marketing and sales, public relations, and contracting, and negotiated lodge rates with tour operators from all over the world. I was so pleased that these men with investments in the business entrusted me with this responsibility. Three of them were members of the prestigious Young Presidents Association in South Africa, and they were great to work with. Their faith in me encouraged me to be self-motivational, so I took the company to another level. We did very well.

Chapter 4

Starting Over In America

*M*y health almost back to normal and my professional career going well, I was happy. Everything was hunky-dory. I had wonderful friends and wasn't in any hurry to form a permanent romantic relationship. My dream always had been to get married and have a family, but there was plenty of time for that, and I had become quite career-oriented. You reach a stage, however, when you think you can have both: You can have somebody nice, and you can have a career. I thought that would happen to me. It wasn't too long before I met a man whom I looked upon as a potential husband. The relationship went well for a while, but then started to deteriorate and became hard to manage. I began to realize, probably subconsciously, that this person was possessed of some unsettling traits. The worst thing was, he wanted to control me. My mother always says, "You can't keep the Smith girls down." I have another mantra for the distaff half of the clan: You can't keep the Smith girls bound. This guy seemed obsessed with claiming ownership over me, like stock in General Motors—make that Ford.

My family and friends could see that the relationship was not good, but I was emotionally involved—in fact, I loved him—and was unable, or unwilling, to look at the situation rationally. But then, what person caught up in the throes of romance does? The old saw has always had it right: Love is blind. My eyesight was nearly back to normal, but on this issue, my vision was skewed.

Meanwhile, my mother and stepfather traveled again to Lexington, Kentucky, to check out racehorses. They arrived on the Fourth of July, 1994, and everybody was celebrating, with firecrackers popping throughout the warm, sunny day, and then fireworks bursting against the night sky in spectacular showers of glittering colors accompanied by sonic booms. And she thought this was a wonderful place to be. So she and her husband entered a drawing of the USA Green Card Lottery, which awards green cards to fifty-five-thousand people each year. It had been her dream to retire in South Africa and then emigrate to the United States. They won, and moved here shortly afterward, settling in Boca Raton, Florida.

My relationship, which had begun four years earlier, dragged on for another three years, and I was now thirty-four years old. Finally, I yielded to the advice of those close to me and sought counseling. I visited my rabbi, who was a brilliant philosopher and helped me understand what was important in life. Then I had several sessions with a psychologist, who was able to skillfully make me aware of what was going on between my suitor and me. A therapist doesn't tell you directly what he or she sees as the problem, but guides you in such ways that you start seeing it yourself. For example, my counselor would present a hypothetical relationship and ask what I would do if I knew of such a situation. And I'd answer, "Oh, I would feel so sorry for this person and say get the hell out of there." And then he would make me understand that I was that person. After a few sessions, I came to realize that I would never have peace of mind in this relationship, and I had to break it off and start a new life. I needed to move on.

This seven-year involvement had a major, stultifying impact on my life. I can't say why I let it happen. In many ways, I am so strong. But in this ill-fated romance, I was weak.

I had watched the African National Congress under Nelson Mandela move against the apartheid National Party and win the first democratic elections in April 1994, resulting in the Government of National Unity, with Mandela as president and the National Party's Frederik Willem de Clerk as his first deputy. It was wonderful to be in South Africa as Mandela presided over the transition from minority rule and apartheid to democracy. But in other respects, things weren't going so well in the country. Robberies, murders and rapes were on the rise, and Johannesburg no longer was a safe place to live.

Everything was coming together and pointing me in one direction: northwest to America. As an only child growing up without a father, I was so close to my mother and missed her greatly in the three years since she had relocated. The insecurity wrought by the increase in crime was putting a crimp in the lifestyles of law-abiding folks in Johannesburg. And I simply had to find a way out of the untenable relationship that I was mired in.

I took advantage of vacation time that I'd earned at Inyati and came here to visit my mother. And I thought, this isn't such a bad place. Upon my return to Johannesburg, I slapped a résumé together and mailed it out to a host of hotels and marketing firms in the United States. Nothing. And I thought, why? Because I'm South African? Maybe because it would be difficult for me to get a Green Card. So I decided, okay, I'm meant to be in South Africa, because I love the country and I love my job and I love the people I work for. And I had wonderful friends.

But then there was the downside—which I couldn't *push* aside. I longed to be near my mother. And I had to break away from the relationship that lingered as a thorn in my side and left me feeling hurt every time we were together. It was like forbidden fruit. I thought, I've just got to get away. Otherwise I'll never have a life.

So, with no job awaiting me, I came to South Florida in August 1997 with the hope of finding one. Lo and behold, I was here only two weeks when something happened. My mother and stepfather, Ivor Marsden, introduced me to Lana Marks, the handbag designer, who is a second cousin of Ivor. She in turn introduced me to Maurice Shawzin, a fellow South African. He just happened to be general manager and director of the Chesterfield Hotel, a cozily intimate, boutique hotel in the quaint European style, perfectly situated in a quiet area of Palm Beach. It is only a stone's throw from famed Worth Avenue, facing a residential section of beautiful but unpretentious, conventional-styled homes imbued with character, the dowry of age, and framed by well-manicured hedges under canopies of towering palms and deciduous trees lushly appointed with mosaics of leaves that dapple the sun's rays.

He said to me, "Maybe we can find a position for you at the hotel." And I said, "Fine, I'll do anything." He gave my résumé to Beatrice Tollman, the president and founder of Red Carnation Hotels. But my visa, valid for only a few weeks, was running out—and besides, I was still working for the game lodge. So I prepared to leave for South Africa.

Two days before my departure date, Mrs. Tollman called and said, "Come and meet me." I drove my mother's car to her house in Palm Beach, not knowing where I was going and heading down the wrong side of the road part of the way, because the driving in South Africa is on the left side. Arriving a bit early, I went into the parking lot of the Greek Orthodox Church to wait. No one could accuse me of trespassing: My great-grandfather was Greek. And what better place to meditate? I thought, *Oh well, it's meant either to be or not to be*, to borrow from The Bard. At the house, a maid led me into the library. Mrs. Tollman entered, and after we chatted, she interviewed me. She made a few calls to persons in South Africa, and they all recommended me highly. I went home, and she called a little while later, saying, "I've spoken to my husband, and I'd like to offer you a job as director of public relations." Back then, the company consisted of only two hotels, the Chesterfield here and one in London. She said the hotels were luxurious and the guests were the well-heeled type I had been accustomed to dealing with at Inyati. The job would be based in London, she added.

And I said, "That's fabulous. I'm so happy that you offered me this position. But I can't take it." A pregnant (that's what this book is about, after all) silence. I hastily added, "Because I love the sun, and in London there is no sun. And also, I wanted to come to America to be near my mother. I'm an only child, and I love my mother a lot. We have a very close bond." I said that I just couldn't go through with it. She said that she understood, and bade me a cordial goodbye.

It was Valentine's Day, and I left for a wedding-anniversary party of my mother and stepdad, Ivor. Arriving late, I was noticed by everyone, and they asked, "Well, how did the interview go?" I said, "Great. I was offered the job, but in London, and I turned it down. And they said, "Are you sure you want to turn this down?" I repeated that I couldn't live in that dismal, cold climate. Little did I know that I later would grow to love London for its inexorable pulse. But regardless of how I felt about living there, the main reason I wanted to leave South Africa was to be near my mother. I told the guests I would fly back to South Africa the next day.

In the morning, the phone rang, and it was Mrs. Tollman. "I've talked to my husband," she said, "and we'd love to have you work for us, and we'll base you out of Palm Beach."

I was elated—and really sad. Because I would have to tell my bosses at Inyati that I was leaving them. It would be quite traumatic. I always get tears in my eyes when I talk about the lodge. It was my baby. I grew with it, and I grew it. But opportunity comes only once or twice, and you have to take advantage of it.

"That's wonderful," I told Mrs. Tollman.

As I had expected, my bosses at Inyati were very upset. But I continued working there eight months, allowing them plenty of time to find a successor, while the entangled legal process of obtaining a work permit so I could renew my visa played out. The Tollmans waited. I was very lucky. If it weren't for them, I wouldn't be here.

Finally, in August 1997, I came to America and settled in with my mother and Ivor in Boca Raton, where I lived for a year before moving to a condominium twenty miles north in South Palm Beach. Equipped with the H1B work permit that I had obtained at the American Consulate in Johannesburg, I began working for Red Carnation. The Tollmans had acquired a second hotel in London, and were in the process of acquiring the Rubens Hotel, across from Buckingham Palace. I was due to fly there August 14 to meet with Mrs. Tollman and see the Montague in Bloomsbury, the Chesterfield in Mayfair, and the Rubens, all in sections of London. Two days before, my mother and I were sitting in her living room after dinner, watching television in our pajamas and having coffee, when some breaking news interrupted the program: Princess Diana had been involved in a serious car accident in Paris. Later, of course, we learned that she had died. When I arrived, the scene was very touching. The traffic from people who drove slowly by Buckingham Palace, just to show their sorrow, was unbelievable. The flowers at the Palace—it was incredible. Everybody at the hotel was having the traditional tea, and they were all crying and grieving over Lady Di. The city was replete with flowers; Harrod's had a luxuriant profusion of them outside the store. Upon waking the next morning, Sunday, we couldn't hear a pin drop. It was total silence. Everybody was in mourning. All you heard was the periodic peal of church bells. It was a sad experience, but a historical moment that I was caught up in.

And then I returned to Palm Beach and started working. I dove into my job as director of public relations, working sixteen hours a day. Because I discovered that it was a whole different way of life here. You have to work harder. And, knowing no one, I realized that I had to be especially diligent to prove myself. Even though I was very career-oriented in South Africa, I had to start over again here. I had to start from scratch. And that was tough. Before, I was a big fish in a small pond, and now I was a small fish in a big pond. I was young and a foreigner. What did I know? I learned that in the American system, you had to learn the politics and bureaucracy of the business world. I think every company has it. In South Africa, we didn't have that competitive intrigue quietly and insidiously fermenting beneath the surface—at least not in my experience. Businesses seemed to operate more openly and directly, with less behind-the-scenes maneuvering. The demands of one's job and the competition for advancement were not so intense as here, where you either get going or get pushed off the tracks. You have to fight all the way to keep your job: There are no guarantees. You live this life of insecurity, feeling constant pressure to prove yourself. Eventually, your work takes control of your life, and you become a workaholic. South Africa's culture is quite similar to that of Europe—more vibrant, with a less-spartan work ethic. In South Africa, your life has balance. You have a career, but you have a social life, too.

Mom knows all too well what kind of regimen I follow: "She will work from about eight o'clock in the morning till nine at night, come home, have something to eat, and then go back on the computer until the wee hours of the morning. In South Africa, you work eight to five and that's it."

Truth be told, though, with a genetic disposition that is highly competitive, I adapted well to the American system. I worked really, really hard, and after several years was promoted to vice president for public relations for the whole company by my boss, Brett Tollman, the Tollmans' son. He's brilliant, and a good person.

Meanwhile, my mother obtained her United States citizenship in 1999, and shortly thereafter I acquired my Green Card.

A few weeks after the terrorist attacks of September 11, 2001, I was sent to Europe for a sales trip that lasted six to eight weeks. Traveling all over the continent by myself, I was a little apprehensive, but managed to make a number of valuable contacts and stimulate considerable interest in the brand. My schedule was so chock-full that I kept my hair very short because I didn't have time to fuss with it each day before traveling. I became very driven—not so much to advance my career as to vent the passion I had for my work and the belief I had in the hotels. You have to love what you do and be self-motivated in order to fully exploit your potential. Working for the Tollmans is a joy.

Around the turn of 2005, Mrs. Tollman said, "How about coming to London every two weeks?" She thought better results would come from our public relations efforts in London if we conducted them ourselves and ceased paying a PR firm in London to do the job. The company had been adding hotels and now has thirteen: eight in England—six in London, one in Dorset, and one in Guernsey; one in Geneva; three in South Africa; and one in Palm Beach. All are ranked high by rating organizations. With such a large presence in England, a closer personal involvement was needed, Mrs. Tollman felt. She expressed confidence that I could handle the job.

So that's what I've been doing ever since, adjusting to the five-hour time difference. I had been working on the media in the United States, and expanded my efforts to the British media. Working with the American media has been fabulous; they're very outgoing and spontaneous. The British media are different. You have to take your time. It's all about respect and relationships. It's more formal and regimented, but it's fun. And the British assignment presented a challenge, opening new doors for me. All the while, London gradually grew on me, and I now am in love with the city.

Chapter 5

The Big Decision

When I first came to live in America, romantic relationships weren't very important for me. I was so hurt by my breakup with my boyfriend in South Africa that, after years, reflecting on it is still unsettling for me. That relationship took the best years of my life. I was so young, and might have met someone with whom I could have had a marriage and family. And I didn't. I really messed that up. In my public relations work, I go to a lot of cocktail and charity events, and meet people. Some of them lined me up with a few blind dates after I had settled into Palm Beach. I especially remember two doctors and an attorney. Nice people, but there was no connection. These men don't want strong women. And on the phone, they want your whole life history before they meet you. Then, when they do meet you, they say, "Oh, so you travel a lot. You're not available." After a while, I pretended I was a concierge in a hotel. I didn't tell them what I really did, and it made a difference. They didn't feel so threatened.

But it's true that I was traveling a lot—every two weeks to London, loving it. So I didn't have a chance to meet a lot of men, and certainly none of whom I could say, "Wow, he's for me. I could spend my whole life with him and go to bed at night with him and wake up in the morning with him." I'm surrounded by people—those I meet in my overseas travels, and some in Palm Beach society circles—and have made many great friends. But I've never met a man I really wanted to get close to.

Nonetheless, I never gave up on my dream—you know, boy meets girl and they have a family and settle down, and all those nice things. I wanted to be a part of the tradition that has molded human society throughout history. Maybe it's because, growing up without a father, I unconsciously felt that I had missed out on an important element of life, even though I was raised in a loving environment.

So, never having realized personal fulfillment, I was particularly disheartened by the results of a medical checkup that I had in early 2004. Over the years, I had annually visited my gynecologist for a Pap smear that women routinely undergo to determine if any cell changes have occurred in the cervix. This time, my gynecologist, Dr. Geoffrey Zann, discovered that I had precancerous cells caused by a human papilloma virus (HPV) infection. I remember that I felt betrayed. He performed a colposcopy to get a magnified look at the cervix, and the results were unfavorable. A second one on the same day produced the same findings. Then he did a scraping of the endocervical canal, which was uncomfortable, so I tried to distract myself by chatting away with him about life and politics. When the results of the scraping came back, Dr. Zann decided they weren't so abnormal as to warrant further action.

A year later, I returned for another Pap smear. The results were not good, nor were those of a following colposcopy.

"I'm cursed by the angels, just cursed," I exclaimed. Dr. Zann did another scraping, with similar findings. "Arnelle," he said, "I'm doing everything I can. I'm trying to maintain it." And I answered, "You have to. I want to have children. I really want to have children. So what do I do?"

"Look," he said, "you can carry on doing these procedures and continue monitoring it, or you can go to an oncologist."

This was not what I had envisioned in my life. I had a plan, and a goal. You have to set goals for yourself. It's very important. I always have. I wanted to have a family. But it just wasn't happening. And time was running out. I had turned forty-two several months earlier.

So I sat down with my mom and said, "I'd like to have a baby. How do you feel about it?" And she said, "I'm fine with it."

So I said, "One has to work out the logistics and be logical. Bringing a life into this world is a big responsibility, and you have to take care of it and nurture it, and it's expensive, not cheap. You've got to cuddle it, feed it, school it. You've got to take care of that baby till it's twenty-one, and after that it's on its own in the world. But even after twenty-one, you still take care of it."

My mother must have thought, "Are you just now figuring all of that out? What do you suppose I did for you all those growing-up years—and beyond?" But all she said was, "I'm fine. I'm happy about it. Go with it if you can."

We thought it over some more, and I proposed to Mom that I pay her to help me look after the baby. She readily agreed to that, even though she was working for a company from seven a.m. to eight at night every day, even Saturdays. She would be the granny nanny.

But I thought, *I don't know how to go about this.* I discussed my plan with Linda, my assistant, and with Corinne, a close friend in London, and they provided helpful input and support. In vitro fertilization, I decided—that's the only way to do it. The procedure was first performed in July 1978 by Patrick Steptoe and Robert Edward in the United Kingdom, and an uproar ensued over its safety and morality. That didn't stop Dr. Subhash Mukhopadhyay from attempting it a few months later in India, a nation of much stricter religious orientation. He successfully produced the first test tube baby in India. But the physician paid a big penalty for his courage. He was reprimanded, socially ostracized, and denied permission by the government to attend international conferences. Mukhopadhyay committed suicide in 1981. I owe him a lot, because his sacrifice encouraged others to turn out IVF babies: one in 1980 in Melbourne, Australia; and in 1981, the first one in the United States, in Norfolk, Virginia. Its popularity rapidly increased after that, with well over 115,000 born in this country.

But with only about one percent of all births now conceived in vitro, it still is a fairly radical way to have a baby, and was even more so in 2005 than today. And while we're throwing statistics around, here's one I wasn't aware of—one that might have discouraged me from attempting IVF. Of women over forty who attempted the procedure in recent years, only 11.5 percent were able to give birth. So I was a lucky one out of about nine. I think it must have been my overwhelming desire to have a baby. I willed it.

Before I could proceed with my plan to have the baby, I needed to deal with the cancer issue. I told Dr. Zann, "I love you, you're fabulous, and you've done a wonderful job. But I think maybe I should follow your suggestion and seek the opinion not just of an oncologist, but one who specializes in my condition." He agreed, and a friend of mine recommended Dr. Howard Goodman in West Palm Beach, who was lecturing extensively on cervical cancer, human papilloma virus, and related issues. He has been informing people about a new vaccine, Gardasil, promoted by experts, that can be administered to adolescent girls before they engage in sexual intercourse to prevent them from contracting HPV.

In April of that year, 2005, I went to see Dr. Goodman, who did a PAP smear to test for the presence of cancer in my cervix and sent it to a laboratory. The results came back negative, but he wanted to be sure, and sent me to a more specialized lab while consulting with other doctors. I sat down with him and said, "I just want to have this baby. Give me a chance to have this baby. That's all I want to do."

His response: "I'm going to give you a time frame. I want you to go and have that baby. Do it." What he meant was that if cancer were found, surgery to remove my reproductive parts would be required and I never would be able to have a baby. So I couldn't wait much longer; I would have to become impregnated within a few months. After that, monitoring for the possible presence of cancer would not be possible until after the baby's birth because the hormones would interfere with testing.

So I went back to Dr. Zann and said, "I'm going to do it." He said, "Fine, but you have to have tests to determine whether you're able to have a baby."

The first test was to check the condition of my fallopian tubes. A catheter was inserted into my vagina and guided up through the cervix into the uterus. The pain was excruciating because of the sensitivity of my cervix caused by the scraping.

But the radiologist had difficulty getting the catheter positioned where he could inject dye into the two fallopian tubes, which are situated on either side of the uterus. It took him fourteen minutes, and the pain was awful. The dye showed that the one tube was perfectly good but the other one was blocked. Dr. Zann referred me to a fertility specialist in Jupiter, Dr. Gene Manko.

After I explained to Dr. Manko my background and the history of what had transpired, he said, "You know, you're mad. Why are you doing this? You're playing with your life. You're planting a time bomb."

"I've just got to try it," I said. "I have to try it and see if I can do it, if it will work."

But he was against it because I had those precancerous cells flaring, and my age was against me. He asked again, "Are you sure you want to do this? You're playing with fire."

Assured that I was determined to proceed, he finally said, "Okay, if that's what you want, fine."

He didn't have much choice. I'd already contacted male friends in South Africa about my plan, and asked if they would be willing to be donors if I could assure them that they would bear no responsibility for the baby. I explained that I wanted several donors so no one would know whose sperm was used in the fertilization. That way, no one would be beholden. I had known the men whom I asked for a number of years, and all agreed, saying it would be a pleasure to bestow this gift on me. Another reason for having multiple donors was that I would have nothing to hide from my child. It didn't concern me that he or she would never know who the father was. That, perhaps more than anything, is what pleases me about writing this book: Shaelah will know there are no secrets.

After arranging for the donors, I contacted my gynecologist in Johannesburg, who referred me to a fertility clinic with several doctors. We held a teleconference to discuss the possible outcomes of an in vitro procedure. The head nurse at the clinic told me I would have to undergo tests to determine whether my eggs were fertile and my internal productive organs—the ovaries and the uterus—were normal.

So I returned to Dr. Manko for blood tests, and laparoscopic surgery to check out the ovaries and uterus. For that procedure, a scope is passed through the navel. One of the fallopian tubes, through which the egg passes from the ovary to the uterus, was blocked, and he had to unblock it. I watched the whole thing on video. It was incredible. All of these organs are so close together that it's no wonder cancer spreads from one to another. I also had extensive endometriosis, the spread of material from the endometrium, or mucous membrane surrounding the uterus, to other organs. That condition precludes pregnancy, and Dr. Manko removed these cysts with the laparoscopic procedure. As for the other tests, they determined that my eggs were developing well.

"You're ready to go to South Africa," he proclaimed.

Chapter 6

Crisscrossing the Continents

I telephoned the fertility doctors, and they instructed me to begin taking a particular tablet to stimulate my egg-production cycle. It's all scientifically planned out, and I carefully followed the schedule they had set up. After all, I didn't want to fly all the way to South Africa and then lay an egg, so to speak. My mother accompanied me as, feeling very excited, we took off on the sixteen-hour journey, flying from the West Palm Beach airport to Miami and from there to Dakar, Senegal, on Africa's west coast, for refueling before continuing to Johannesburg.

The flight had been delayed, so when we landed, our family friend Maree Van Vuuren, with whom we stayed during the visit, took us straight from the airport to the hospital for an injection that fertilizes the eggs and makes them ripen more quickly. The following morning, I returned for a scan to measure the size of the two eggs, one in each ovary. When a follicle—a vesicle, or little pouch, in the ovary that contains a developing egg—is twenty or twenty-two, they can give an injection to trigger the release of the eggs. I was ready, and the eggs were triggered. The concluding step would be to implant the sperm, which, I was told, would be thawed, cleaned and rinsed, then placed in a catheter and injected into the cervix. But before returning for this final procedure, the nurse told me, I would have to see a counselor for a psychological evaluation. I was stupefied. Wasn't it a little late for this? But, having no choice, off I went the next morning with my mother and Marie for a visit with this psychologist appointed by the clinic to evaluate prospective recipients of in vitro fertilization.

The woman asked, "Well, why do you want to have a baby and be a single mother?"

"You know," I replied, "time is ticking, and I have precancerous cells that could turn into cancer and require a hysterectomy, which would prevent me from having a baby later. I'm getting older. I've had a wonderful career. I've traveled all over the world. I've done a lot of good things in my life. And I have no regrets. Now I can settle down—and enjoy having a baby. But I haven't met somebody I'd like to have one with. If I had, it would have been great. So I want to do it. And financially, I can take care of the baby."

And she said, "I don't understand. You should be married."

"I'd rather be on my own than be with somebody just for the sake of it," I retorted, trying not to sound irritated. "So many married people are unhappy. I come from a divorced home. My mom and dad got divorced when I was two years old. My mother wanted me to be a happy child. Why must you marry for the sake of marrying and be with somebody you're going to be unhappy with and your child's going to be unhappy? And I have maternal instincts. So that's the way I want it to be. I want to have a child by myself."

The reasons I gave were solid, logical answers. I had been thinking through the process so it would benefit the child.

The psychologist finished the evaluation and said she would forward it to the doctors. She was very nice to me.

My appointment with the doctor the next day was at nine a.m., so I had to drive through rush-hour traffic to get there. Johannesburg's traffic had become awfully crowded at peak times due to overpopulation and improved economic conditions that put more cars on the road. People who never had owned a car now had one. And the truck traffic was unbelievable. But my mother and I didn't mind. We were ecstatic, knowing that the big event finally was going to happen. At last we arrived at the doctor's office.

Here's Mom: "We were so excited we could hardly contain ourselves. Even in the car, were like little children."

Indeed, we were like kids playing—singing and laughing and talking. At the office, we waited, and in a short while the clinic's head nurse called us into her office.

"We can't go through with this," she said.

It was as though I'd been struck by lightning. I sat there and stared at the woman with my mouth open, unable to speak. Then, "What are you talking about? What do you mean?" I was becoming hysterical. I couldn't believe this. The nurse told us that the counselor, who had charged me three-hundred-fifty Rand (about sixty dollars), advised her that it was not good for me to be a single mother. It had never even occurred to me that she might say such a thing—not in the twenty-first century. Single mothers abound in today's world.

Mom: "Arnelle collapsed. She started crying and sobbing."

The injections to trigger release of the eggs already had been done, and the process was under way. Mom told the nurse: "If she doesn't have the sperm injected now, she'll have to come back to Africa again later. We made all of these plans, carried out all the necessary procedures in advance, and flew all the way from South Florida to South Africa. And you're telling us it was all for nothing?"

We were emotionally destroyed, and it was obvious to the nurse, who sympathized. So, handing me a tube containing the sperm, she said, "Why don't you take this? Keep it between your hands. You have to keep the sperm warm. Go home and buy a syringe and inseminate yourself."

So we went straight to a pharmacist and bought a syringe of the kind that the nurse had described, and returned to the home of Marie Van Vuuren, the friend we were staying with.

Mom vividly remembers what happened next: "We inseminated her with the syringe, and she had to lie with her legs up. And I looked at her in that bed, with her head at the foot and her legs resting on the headboard. I was so sad because she looked so lonely. So I kicked my shoes off and lay down beside her and put my legs up. We laid there for two hours. And our friend's maid, Betty, and butler, Solly, were running around, bringing things for us to eat and making sure we were comfortable. They were all upset for Arnelle."

Marie said her son and daughter-in-law, Nickie, might know a good fertility doctor—a specialist in the same clinic to which her gynecologist belonged. We called Nickie, and she said that, yes, she knew of a fantastic one. His name was Dr. Hennie Lindeque, and she made an appointment for us with him the next day.

"What were they doing to you?" my mother remembers him asking incredulously.

Dr. Lindeque said he wanted to check with a friend who was a professor of law on the legality of in vitro fertilization in my circumstances. He made a phone call, and told us it was perfectly legal for me to have the procedure. So I said, "Great. Now can we do it?"

He did a scan to determine the size of the eggs and found they had shrunk and dropped. The insemination had to be done within two days after the eggs were triggered, he said. I told him I had inseminated myself.

"Are you crazy?" he exclaimed. "You could injure yourself so badly. It's really wrong to do it that way." He talked about how some women tried to self-inseminate by reading instructions in a book. They even used a champagne bottle to make the injection, he said.

So I told him, "Maybe what I did will work."

In the next couple of days, before we returned to Florida, the counselor called me on my cell phone and said, "I'm so sorry, Arnelle, that I gave you that evaluation." She apparently had thought it over and realized she'd made a mistake.

But I was in no forgiving mood. In fact, I was furious. "How dare you phone and tell me you're sorry that you told the doctors I had no right to be a single parent?" I said vehemently. "I'm not ready? I'm not right? Who gives you the right to control my life? I should not be a single parent? You're not my destiny. I'm my own destiny. How dare you try to control my life?" I was hysterical.

"You'll live with this for the rest of your life," I upbraided her, my voice rising to a decibel level it never had reached in all my years of dramatic acting.

We came back home to Florida, and the insemination didn't take. So we had to start all over again. Dr. Lindeque said I had to wait for my next monthly reproductive cycle to begin and start taking the prescribed tablets immediately upon its onset, continuing to swallow them for four days. Then I had to administer my own injections to fertilize the eggs and facilitate their ripening. Back in the Palm Beaches, Dr. Manko's nurse taught me the procedure: Draw the fluid into a large needle, transfer it into a smaller needle, and inject through the navel. I would have to do it once at home and another time on the plane en route to South Africa. The entire procedure was highly regimented.

The first injection didn't go so well. I'll let Mom describe it:

"We were so excited—I don't know what—that we forgot to change to the smaller needle. And Arnelle stuck the big needle in, and you could hear the skin breaking. It went through the skin into the tissue. We looked at each other with big eyes as if to say, 'Oh, my God.'"

It was painful but, in unorthodox fashion, we accomplished our objective, even though we felt like the Three Stooges minus one. The next day, I boarded the plane with my mother, carrying the needle with the fluid in my purse. If I'd have tried that these days, a couple of crew-cut, muscular guys wearing dark suits and dark glasses would have stopped me at the check-in line, whisked me away to a windowless room, sat me down on a small, wooden chair under a bright light, and given me the third degree for several hours. I can just picture it:

"But you don't understand. I was just planning to fertilize my eggs. You have to believe me." A rolling of the eyes. "Sure, lady, we believe you. And then you were going to start a chicken farm, right?" Yuk yuk yuk. "Sorry, Maam, but we're going to have to lock you up while we get to the bottom of this."

During the flight, I went to the rest room and injected myself. We arrived on a Saturday, and I injected myself again, then went to see Dr. Lindeque. He did a scan and found the eggs were sized sixteen and eighteen, and said they should be twenty by the next day and perfect by Monday. That day, the eggs measured twenty and twenty-two. The technicians washed the sperm and placed it in the catheter. Because of the several procedures I'd undergone to rid my cervix of the precancerous cells, Dr. Lindeque had difficulty inserting the catheter. He finally had to push through the uterus wall, which was excruciatingly painful for me. My friend in the waiting room could hear me screaming. After ten minutes, the pain went away, and I was led to a stretcher, where the nurses made me warm and comfortable. Dr. Lindeque sent me home with the directive that I have a blood test on the tenth day. He said that I could do whatever I wanted, that I didn't need to restrict my physical activity—which I thought was amazing.

By then it was early November (2005), and the festive spirit of the approaching holiday season was incipient, so I went with my mother and a group of friends to Miami for a weekend-long, fiftieth birthday party of a friend named Arthur. He was the host and had chosen the hotel where everybody was to stay.

"Isn't this hotel fantastic?" he casually asked me. And I responded, "I don't think it's that great."

Arthur took my mother aside and asked, "What's the matter with Arnelle? I've never seen her like this, so aggravated. She normally would never say that?" And Mom replied, "Oh, this is good. It could be a sign that she's pregnant. That's one of the symptoms." He was the only one at the party to whom I had divulged my intention to have a baby.

Back at home the next day, Sunday, I bought a home pregnancy test from a drug store, and the results were negative. I wasn't pregnant. Driving to work Monday, I debated whether to have a blood test done professionally, and went to a Quest Diagnostics laboratory in West Palm Beach the next day. On the following day, Eileen, Dr. Manko's head nurse, called me and said she had the results.

"You're pregnant."

"What?" I shouted joyfully. "I cannot believe this." Even though the people at the South African fertility clinic had told me I was quite fertile, especially for my age, I had deliberately lowered my expectations of becoming expectant to soften the crushing disappointment if it didn't happen.

"Well, we're shocked ourselves," Eileen said. "We find it hard to believe."

Not only had I not told many of my friends about my plans to procreate, but I also had not disclosed to my boss what I was doing. Considering the inflexibility of the modern business world, I figured, one could not be certain of the reaction to news of one's pregnancy. I decided not to tell anyone except the few friends to whom I had disclosed my plans and, of course, my mother, who was thrilled, as was Dr. Lindeque when I phoned him. Everyone was ecstatic, including my oncologist Dr. Goodman, who motivated me to have the baby. I can't say enough about him—a great doctor, very precise, never recommending surgery unless it's really necessary.

Chapter 7

Devastated

$\mathcal{E}$ight weeks later, on Dec. 28, I was driving to my office at The Chesterfield in Palm Beach, heading north on South County Road. I was happy. The celebratory mood of the holidays was in the air, and snowbirds were returning to their winter homes to begin the season of charitable galas and endless partying. Gentle breezes wafted in from the Atlantic Ocean only a block away, and it was a beautiful, balmy, sunshiny day. The fetus was living up to the nickname we'd assigned her: "the dolphin," because she would jump this way and that inside me, bumping against the uterine wall.

Suddenly my ebullience was aborted by a much heavier bump, this one from the outside, at the left rear side of my two-door coupe, a Mercedes 230C. I didn't even see what hit me, but found myself careening into an electric-power pole off the right side of the road. Boom! I hit it head-on. The airbags burst out, thank God, and I smelled something burning. I was able to get out of the car, and a young man approached. Driving a Budget rental van, he had turned left from Jungle Road onto South County Road, apparently without looking

"I didn't see you," he said.

"I don't believe it," I shouted. "I'm pregnant, I'm pregnant."

"Oh, I'm sorry," he said, and I asked, "What were you thinking?" He answered that the sun had blinded him, but I didn't believe that, either, and neither did the police. He was a young fellow from Toronto, a worker at one of those beautiful homes that grace the narrow strip of land called Palm Beach, between the Atlantic and the Intracoastal Waterway.

The crash not only totaled my car, but broke the power pole, cutting off electricity to the homes in the area. A woman emerged from a home on the east side of the road, and I told her I was pregnant. She said she would call the paramedics, and they arrived in minutes. They couldn't believe I was standing there. They thought I should be dead, they said while laying me flat on a board and strapping me down. They drove me in the ambulance to Good Samaritan Hospital in West Palm Beach, on the west side of the Intracoastal.

The doctor told me I would have to undergo a brain scan to see if I were bleeding, and I said, "I can't have a brain scan and I can't have a CAT scan, because I'm pregnant."

He said, "But you should, because you could be bleeding. You're risking your life."

I answered, "I know I'm risking my life. I had a brain aneurysm when I was twenty-three. But that's the chance I'll have to take. I know if I'm not feeling good in my head, and I can't do anything about the back, because a scan might damage the baby."

"You're playing with your life," he warned again, and I said, "I know." I actually was worried that the aneurysm might have ruptured. But then I figured that if I were bleeding, I would feel it, and I would be seeing everything go round and round in colors.

The doctor said, "If that's the way you want it, I can't even X-ray your hand. It's broken." So the nurse bandaged it and I was sent to a specialist in North Palm Beach, a dozen miles away, who determined that the hand would heal properly. While I was still in the hospital, an ultrasound of the fetus was performed, and everything checked out normal. "Fabulous!" I said. "I'm happy." Then several of my friends, whom my mother had called after the paramedics notified her, arrived along with Mom, and we all breathed sighs of relief that everything was going to be okay. I went home and discovered my boss already had been told about the accident, and he was very sympathetic and supportive. My bosses didn't know I was pregnant, but my friends did. In keeping with my wishes, they kept it a secret.

I went to see Dr. Manko the next day, December 29, and he did another ultrasound, which determined that the baby was fine, the heartbeat was good, and it was moving up and down and around.

Two days later, on the day of New Year's Eve, I decided to go with friends for dinner that night at the Palm Beach Yacht Club, across the Intracoastal bridge from Palm Beach, but lay down the whole day because I was a bit apprehensive. At the club, I had a terrible pain in my back, so I went the next day to the hospital, where the doctor found that a disc had popped out. I had to begin physiotherapy immediately.

A week later, I got out of bed in the morning and saw blood gushing out of my uterus. It was like a tap—a gush of blood, then a shut-off, and then another gush. I phoned Dr. Manko, who told me to come immediately to have the fetus checked. I phoned my mother and asked her to take me. It was the worst drive, because my heart was beating wildly with fear for the baby. My mother and I were feeling desperate. The doctor took a scan, and said the heartbeat was normal and everything was okay. As for the bleeding, well, it just happened sometimes in a pregnancy, he said. He thought I might have a bit of a leak, or whatever. We were utterly happy and relieved.

Dr. Manko referred me a week later to Dr. Debra Jones, a perinatalist, or high-risk-pregnancy doctor. It was about five-thirty p.m. that day and getting dark when I finally saw her.

She was very nice, chatting with me and asking me questions, and telling me that I should have the baby at St. Mary's Hospital, a few miles north in West Palm Beach, because it had an excellent obstetrics department. Even though I'd already had two ultrasound scans to check on the baby a week earlier, Dr. Jones wanted to be sure no complications from the accident had occurred in the meantime.

During the week after the accident, the baby had felt fine inside me, except that it wasn't quite as active as it had been before the accident, when it tossed and turned this way and that.

Dr. Jones had another scan done. When it was finished, the nurse said, "Wait a moment." Then Dr. Jones came into the room and said, "Arnelle, I need to speak to you."

I said, "What's wrong?"

"There's no heartbeat."

My own heart skipped a beat as I gasped. I felt like I had died.

"Are you one hundred percent sure?"

She said that she was. She called Dr. Manko and made an appointment for me the next morning. He told me a D&C, or dilation and curettage, would have to be done. In this procedure, the entrance to the uterus would be expanded (dilation) so that a thin, sharp instrument could be used to scrape or suction away the dead fetus (curettage).

I phoned my mother and she drove up from Boca Raton. I told her, "I don't believe them. There are miracles." I returned to Good Samaritan Hospital and asked for another scan to be certain whether the fetus was dead. I cried and cried and cried. I was devastated. They did the test and confirmed that the baby was dead. I walked around and cried my eyes out. Mom came to my apartment that night, a Thursday, and we cried together, and hugged and prayed. I couldn't believe what had happened.

Here's Mom: "I was devastated along with Arnelle, but tried to put up a brave front, telling her everything would be okay—that we would just have to start over. But when I was alone, I wept over and over."

Next morning, Friday, I went to see Dr. Manko and told him I was flying the following day to London for my regular two weeks of work there. His wife, Linda, who also is his assistant, said, "We're not doing the D&C today, then. You'll bleed to death up there in the airplane." So I said, "Okay, then, I won't go." They rolled me into the operating room, anesthetized me, and removed the fetus through the uterus.

I decided the next day to fly to London. I had to. I'd spent forty-eight hours crying. I said to Mom, "I need to work—to get my mind occupied. I need to move on and put this behind me." But I'm not stupid: If I had felt that something was awry, I would have canceled. I have a positive outlook. One must never be too negative, I feel, but never too positive, either, so as to avoid major disappointments. I was fine on the flight, and none of the people I worked with in London knew what had happened. None had even known about my pregnancy. They knew only that I had been in a car accident.

I returned home two weeks later, but had to wait four months before attempting in vitro fertilization again. Finally, in May (2006), I telephoned the clinic in South Africa. Dr. Lindeque was away, so Dr. Andre Viljoen would see me, I was told. I received the same instructions as before for taking the medication and giving myself injections. I arrived on a Saturday.

"Here we go again," said my friend, Marie Van Vuuren. She was fantastic throughout my travails. I went straight to the clinic for an injection to fertilize the eggs and speed up their ripening. Dr. Viljoen told me to return on the coming Monday to determine whether I was ready for the insemination.

"I'm not sure if I'm looking at the egg or a cyst," he said, referring to one egg that was a bit small. The other was large, a twenty-two or twenty-three. Twins could result from an egg that big. "Because you've come all this way," the doctor said, "we're going to try. We have nothing to lose. But I don't guarantee it."

Besides practicing medicine in South Africa, Dr. Viljoen administered a hospital in Bahrain. He had a sizable reputation.

So off I went the following day for the insemination. I screamed in pain as the catheter was pushed into the cervix. The next day, I flew home and followed the instruction to wait ten days and then have Dr. Manko test to determine if I were pregnant. The nurse, Eileen, phoned me the next day with the bad news: It hadn't worked. Dr. Manko then told me that the small object Dr. Viljoen had referred to probably was, as he had suspected, a cyst. A cyst prevents pregnancy by blocking the sperm swimming toward the egg, Dr. Manko said.

A month passed, but I decided to wait longer before making another attempt. I said to myself, "I'm going to wait for my body to settle first." Shortly before my cycle was scheduled to begin in July, I went to Dr. Manko to determine whether the cyst was still there. It was gone. I realized then that I should have asked before going to South Africa in May that a check for cysts be made.

Once again, I notified Dr. Lindeque that I was coming, and started the routine with the tablets and the injections. I was getting good at this. In fact, if I'd wanted to do drugs instead of birth a baby, I would have made pushers look like pansies, mainliners like mamby-pambies. Off I flew for the fourth time to Johannesburg. The day after I arrived,

Dr. Lindeque said there were two eggs, sized sixteen and eighteen, and he hoped they would be twenty and twenty-two by the next day. Indeed, they were bigger, and the ritual of washing the sperm and preparing it—something akin to getting dinner ready—was performed.

I knew, of course, about the agony I faced because of the surgical procedures that had made my uterus especially pain-sensitive. But I kept thinking, it's for a good cause. I know it's worth it. You've just got to hang in there. I was willing to suffer intense pain to make the greatest contribution any human can give: the gift of life.

Dr. Lindeque couldn't get the catheter inserted properly because of my altered cervix, and had to push it through the uterus. Sure enough, the pain was terrible. That's the way it is: No pain, no gain. But I did it.

Dr. Lindeque was feeling badly for me, because it was the third time I'd undergone the excruciatingly painful insemination at his clinic. He said, "Your eggs are good, and everything looks good. But it's costing you money going back and forth."

He didn't realize that it would have cost me a lot more to do it in this country. Because of the exchange rate of the dollar versus the rand at the time, the cost was about twelve-hundred dollars for each in vitro procedure. I think it would have cost between five thousand and ten thousand here. Of course, I also had to pay the air fares. But I had a friend to stay with, Marie, and had no lodging expenses.

She and I discussed what to do if I didn't become pregnant this time. Should I try one more time? Should I have the insemination done in America, using sperm from a sperm bank? The Food and Drug Administration wouldn't allow importation of sperm from South Africa because the donor had to be tested for AIDS and other medical conditions.

In the evening, Marie prepared a sumptuous dinner for me and invited her whole family. Such camaraderie made for a very pleasant visit every time I went to South Africa, despite the ordeal I underwent each time. I got to see a few friends whom I trusted implicitly, and they were a cushion for me. However, I didn't want all of them to know what I was doing, so I refrained from contacting some who might, I thought, want to know who the sperm donors were. I told all but those few persons that the donor was an anonymous supplier to a sperm bank in America, where I was having the in vitro fertilization performed. I figured that discretion was the prudent policy in dealing with this issue, rather than disclosing my activities to everybody whom I wanted to tell. Everything was so complicated, and the more people who were involved, the more complicated it would become.

The next night, Marie took me to see a show at a performing arts center in Johannesburg. In keeping with South African tradition, we took a picnic basket and wine, while some ordered from restaurants. The show was *Billy Elliot the Musical*, from the 2000 British film *Billy Elliott*, which was adapted for the stage in 2005 and reproduced for a hugely successful run on Broadway that began in 2009. It was produced in Johannesburg by Richard Loring, a native of Britain who had emigrated to South Africa decades before and gained a sizable reputation in the theater. I worked with his wife, Jeanette Stuart, back in my modeling days.

It was a quite pleasant experience, and while watching the show, I had a good feeling about everything. It just came over me.

After the insemination, I had to take a tablet to make the uterus lining thicker so it would hold the baby if I became pregnant. The next day, I said to Marie, "Let's cross our fingers."

She said, "I hope it works. Otherwise, your room is waiting for you upstairs." She'd made the room warm for me because it was July—winter in South Africa, colder than winters in Florida. Jack Frost. I saw snow about four times when I lived there. But it's the best weather in the world.

I left with the form that I needed for a blood test to determine whether I was pregnant, and was happy to be in Palm Beach again. It's a crazy place, but there's something indefinably attractive about it. It's funny that every time I go away, I'm excited to come home.

Chapter 8

A New Life

I had the blood test done, and Eileen, Dr. Manko's nurse, phoned me the next day.

"Arnelle, you're pregnant!" she exclaimed.

Of course I was elated. But I wasn't terribly surprised. I'd left Johannesburg in an ebullient spirit, trying not to be too optimistic but unable to squelch the feeling that this was going to work.

"We can't believe it," Eileen said. You are absolutely incredible. You've been through so much."

I telephoned Dr. Lindeque and related the wonderful news. I wanted to shout it from the rooftops, but decided it would be judicious to wait until after the first trimester of the pregnancy before spreading the word to others. So I called my mother and said, "We're not going to tell anybody."

But I did want to notify my boss, because I had told him I was making the trip to South Africa for the in vitro procedure. He had, after all, telephoned me when I had the car accident and sent me gifts and condolences.

"You remember when I had the car accident?" I asked him. "Well, I was pregnant at the time and lost the baby."

He said, "Oh, my God!"

I was thrilled to be pregnant. It was such a huge relief to me.

On the way to work the next day, I avoided South County Road, as I had done since the accident. I was so scared. It was a weird feeling.

Then I flew to London for my regular two weeks of work. Those jaunts always entailed a lot of meetings over cocktails, and the people I met with didn't understand why I wouldn't drink alcohol. I was hoping they didn't think I was on the wagon, which would have made them wonder whether I'd been a wino all this time.

From London, I had to fly to Geneva, Switzerland, where a really fine London restaurant, Tamarin, did a promotion for us each year. The people of Geneva love Indian food, and Tamarin sponsored a festive curry evening. It's spicy, of course, and would endanger the fetus. I was sitting with my colleagues, and told them, "I'm trying not to eat curry. I've been dieting."

I returned to Palm Beach, and two weeks later was off again to London. The pregnancy was not showing much yet. A colleague, David, invited me to a concert by the Rolling

Stones. It was in Twickenham, a London suburb, and we had to take a train. There must have been a million people at the show in the huge Twickenham Stadium. I stood for about two hours at a cocktail party beforehand, and then we had to walk from the train station to the stadium. Finally, thank God, we sat down for the show, which was terrific. But afterward, it was another trudge back to the station, and I was so tired that it felt like I was walking in mud. At the station, we waited hours to catch a train back to the city. Back at the hotel, I lay down, phoned my mother and told her I was exhausted. Nobody had known I was pregnant.

Back home, Dr. Manko indicated he could do an ultrasound a limited number of times as the pregnancy progressed, and then I would need to see Dr. Jones, the perinatalist, and Dr. Ronnie Koch, an obstetrician, who was recommended by Dr. Goodman. Jones and Koch worked together in separate locations. Dr. Jones would check the baby's heartbeat, have me weighed and do the ultrasounds, and forward the results to Dr. Koch, who would repeat the procedures. The two of them would discuss the outcome of the tests. So I was seeing two doctors. It was all quite comprehensive. Dr. Koch assumed primary responsibility for guiding my pregnancy, and we had a good rapport because he'd been to South Africa on a safari and to visit a friend. Every time I went to see him, he would say, "How*zit?*" That's a common greeting in South Africa. He was knowledgeable about the country and was familiar with its wines, and would tell me stories on every visit.

I must say that I was really fortunate to have such wonderful doctors in Ronnie Koch and Debra Jones. For nine months, they were family, a big part of my life.

Dr. Koch recommended I have a C-section to deliver the baby because the pressure that I would have to apply in a normal delivery could trigger another aneurysm in the brain. He strongly concurred with Dr. Jones' recommendation that I give birth at St. Mary's Hospital, saying, "There really isn't any choice."

Everything went smoothly, and about eighteen weeks into the pregnancy, it was time for me to undergo amniocentesis. This is a test to determine whether any genetic abnormalities exist in the fetus. Testing is most commonly done for Down's syndrome, spina bifida (incompletely formed spinal cord) and Trisomy 18, which refers to extra material from chromosome 18 that interferes with normal development. It affects about one in three thousand births and is three times more common in girls than boys. Younger women are at less risk of giving birth to genetically abnormal children and amniocentesis usually is not performed on them. They merely undergo blood tests.

Before the procedure was scheduled, a genetic checker who visited Dr. Jones' office about once a week asked me about my lineage. I told him it was irrelevant because the sperm donor was anonymous.

In the procedure, a small amount of amniotic fluid, which contains fetal tissues, is extracted through a needle from the amnion, or amniotic sac enveloping the fetus. The DNA from this fluid then is examined for possible abnormalities. Though it is routine, amniocentesis is not without risk, for the puncture of the sac by the needle in a tiny percentage of cases doesn't heal properly, sometimes causing leakage or infection. Serious complications can result in miscarriage.

A local anesthetic sometimes is given to alleviate the pain when the needle is inserted to withdraw fluid, but none was administered to me. Deborah, the nurse, with Dr. Jones, was wonderful to me; we all were like family. Deborah held my hand when I told her that I hated needles. This long needle was punched through my abdomen and on through the wall of the uterus into the amniotic sac. And oh, it was painful.

As Dr. Jones inserted the needle, she and I watched the procedure as it was projected onto a screen via a tiny camera. She saw something awry and said, "Ummm. I'm not happy. I see something on the brain and something on the heart." She said the results from the laboratory testing of the drawn fluid normally were available in ten days to two weeks. However, for an extra three hundred dollars I could have the results three days hence, on that Monday. She had known that I was due to leave for London on Tuesday, and deliberately scheduled the procedure for the preceding Friday so that I would have the necessary recuperation time of several days. I needed to stay on my back and relax, she said.

Of course, I was about as relaxed as a vegetarian at a convention of cannibals. The whole weekend was hell. I just walked around the apartment muttering, "I can't believe this." I didn't want to see anyone.

Finally, I said to my mother, "You know what? If there's something wrong with the baby, I'm just going to abort it. I can't bring a baby into the world if there's something wrong with it. It's a hell of a responsibility. I mean, who looks after it when I'm gone?"

I phoned Dr. Lindeque in South Africa and we had a chat about it. I also phoned Dr. Manko and Dr. Goodman, the top-notch oncologist and specialist in cervical cancer who had advised me to have the in vitro fertilization within months because cancer might occur later and preclude childbirth.

Results of half the tests arrived that Monday, and the doctors said those provided the information they needed to make a determination. All the chromosomes appeared to be okay. Dr. Jones told me that what they had seen on the heart was a bit of crystallization, and a deposit on the right side of the brain would disperse. I was relieved, but still somewhat worried. They said the baby was a girl, and all I said was, "That's fine." It hadn't mattered to me whether the baby were a boy or girl, but I thought a little girl would be nice to have. A frisson radiated through me.

And then off I went to London. Doctors permit pregnant patients to fly up to eight weeks before the delivery date. Brett Tollman, my boss, said he thought I should tell his mother I was pregnant. And I agreed, even though I was anxious about her reaction. I wanted to tell her first, before anyone else found out. Between my meetings, I met her at 41, Red Carnation's five-star hotel on Buckingham Palace Road, ranked No. 1 in England. I sat down and said, "I need to tell you something. I'm pregnant."

"That's wonderful, Arnelle, darling!" she exclaimed. "This is the best news. I'm so happy for you, Arnelle. This is great, and I want to be the granny." I explained to her that I hadn't met the right man so I decided to give birth via in vitro fertilization. And I told her about the hurdles I'd faced—my age and the precancerous condition—in deciding to become pregnant at that time. I also told her about the car accident that ended my first pregnancy.

I told Brett about our meeting, and he said, "See, it wasn't so bad after all."

"Yes," I said, "but I just didn't know how she would take it."

I was so relieved. It was as though a weight had been lifted off my shoulders.

Then I told all of my colleagues in London, and they were thrilled for me and praised me for my courage. I then flew home.

The doctors examined me periodically for how I was faring, especially the condition of my cervix. I developed serious sciatica from the car accident and continued having physiotherapy before the pregnancy advanced to the stage where it was no longer possible. I told my bosses that I had decided to work until the eighth month of pregnancy, and I would not take maternity leave. They were fine with that. In February 2007, a baby shower—a tea—was held for me, and I received the most wonderful gifts from friends, acquaintances, and business associates. There must have been about fifty of them.

But Mom wasn't feeling well at the shower, which was on a Saturday. We thought it might be the flu. By the next Tuesday, her condition had worsened and she went to the emergency room at a hospital in Boca Raton. In my pregnant state, I sat with her as the hospital kept her on a stretcher for forty-eight hours. Finally, I phoned a previous boss of hers at a medical supplies company and pleaded, "You've got to help. My mother is lying on a stretcher and they don't have a room for her. And people are screaming 'Help!' and no one responds."

The executive was away skiing with doctors, all of them big shots from Boca Raton. His office contacted him, and with one phone call he had Mom placed in a room at the hospital. Tests showed that she had an E. coli infection. Further tests revealed a little tumor in the kidney. Complications developed because my mother was on prednisone to correct muscle deterioration called polymyalgia, which was caused by Lipitor that she had taken to counter high cholesterol. She remained hospitalized for two weeks. I didn't think she would be coming out. I kept praying that she would last long enough to see the baby. She was really worried, too, and thought she would never see her grandchild.

But she finally recuperated enough to go home. And what did she do? She went back to working, wedged between antibiotic drips administered by a visiting nurse in the morning and evening. She's crazy. And I thought *I* was crazy. Mom's mantra was proving true: "You can't keep the Smith girls down."

I called a doctor in South Africa, who said it would take two years for the polymyalgia to leave the body, and she would have to gradually wean herself off of the prednisone.

I was reminded of the famous lament by the late Gilda Radner, aka Roseanne Roseannadanna: "It's always somethin'."

Dr. Koch and I had discussed the delivery date for the baby and decided on March 30 because it was a Friday. I could have the C-section, recover for three days and then return to work—but at home, not the office.

The week before, I went in for a stress test, and the movement of the baby wasn't good. I was sent to St. Mary's Hospital for a check on whether the baby was moving a lot. I thought then, "Why don't they just do it now and get it over with?" You know, you worry.

On Thursday, March 29, both Mom and I worked until seven p.m., and she and my stepdad drove the twenty miles from Boca Raton to my condominium in South Palm Beach, where I was living at the time, to stay with me that night. We got up at four in the morning, and I was very excited. Finally my dream was coming true. I was going to give birth to a baby girl. Yahoo! Off we went to St. Mary's Hospital. Drs. Koch and Jones were there, along with three nurses and an anesthesiologist, who administered fluid drips and gave me an epidural to thwart the pain. My mother watched the procedure. I was wide awake and held her hand.

Then the nurses hung a sheet in front of my face so I couldn't watch the C-section birth, which is pretty gory. Dr. Koch made the incision, and they pulled and tugged at the little bundle of life inside me. I could feel only a little sensation.

Dr. Koch said to my mother, "Hey Granma, take a look at your grandchild." My mom, who had been sitting behind the sheet with me, got up and looked, and saw just her head, which was full of muck.

Mom: "It was so weird. I was speechless. Arnelle and I held hands and squeezed with excitement."

I was overwhelmed.

Then Dr. Koch said, "Hold on a minute." The umbilical cord was wrapped around the baby's neck. And I thought, "Thank God I didn't have a regular birth. The baby could have strangled."

They had to unwrap the cord from around the baby's neck, and then they lifted her out and emptied the fallopian tubes and all of the other material and tissue ancillary to the pregnancy.

Mom again: "Then the baby started to scream. And she screamed, and screamed, and screamed. And Arnelle's face just burst into this big smile."

They held her up for me to see, and I couldn't believe it. I looked at my mother and said, "Oh, my God." It was just the most incredible feeling. I cannot explain it.

They reimplanted the parts, and Dr. Koch said, 'Look at this, Granma. Your daughter is so sexy, even her fallopian tubes have got a curve.'"

It was seven-forty-seven in the morning. From that moment, that second, my whole life changed. I entered another chapter, another level, another sphere. One's life metamorphoses.

It was March 30, so close to April Fool's Day. And I fooled everybody.

Epilogue

Postpartum Delight

$\mathcal{A}$fter an orderly wheeled me into the recovery room, a nurse weighed the baby. Eight pounds six ounces. Dr. Goodman called to check if everything was all right. Even Dr. Jones' head nurse, Kim, phoned. They all took a personal interest, as though they were members of my family. It was a wonderful feeling.

Right away, after the nurses had cleaned the baby, they brought her to me and put her in my arms. I immediately began nursing her. I couldn't even feel my legs yet. But after two hours of recovery, I was working on my Blackberry, checking e-mails, and taking phone calls. My mother stayed with me in the hospital for the next three nights.

Three days later, I went home to my condominium. For three months, I worked from home. While Shaelah slept, I worked. Normally, to gain strength, the mother sleeps while the baby sleeps. But I worked right through. I nursed for six months.

Almost thirteen months after the birth, Shaelah and I moved from the cramped condominium in South Palm Beach into a beautiful home in Boca Raton. I didn't pick thirteen on purpose, just as I didn't pick the proximity to April Fool's Day for the birth. They're simply symbolic of the strange twists of fate that have informed my life. But what the heck? I just keep defying the odds.

Like most babies, Shaelah has had her crying bouts, which often metamorphosed instantly into looks of wonder, and just as suddenly a big, joyous smile erupted. I sometimes did a little dance in front of her, and her face lighted up with animation while she waved her little arms to the rhythm. She still climbs onto the piano bench and runs her little fingers over the keyboard. She's going to be a dancer and actress, I think. I have a strong feeling that whatever she becomes, it will be something special.

The move to the much larger home was well-timed. Shaelah was growing, and entered the curious stage, investigating every detail of her new abode. At age three and in pre-school, she has displayed remarkable intelligence and a self-confidence manifested in an eagerness to interact and compete with her peers. Yet she has exhibited a kind and caring attitude toward others

Shaelah is tall for her age and has brown eyes and brown hair. She is picture-postcard pretty. Unlike her mother, who has a dimple on her cheek, Shaelah sports one on her elbow.

Was it all worth it? The utter disappointment and anger at my rejection by the first clinic I visited in Johannesburg? The failure of my self-insemination? The torture of the catheters and needles penetrating the tenderest parts of my body? The shattering blow when my first pregnancy was ended by the car accident?

Every morning when I kiss that little angel goodbye and go off to work, every night when I tuck her into bed, every time she cries and every time she laughs—I have my answer.

###

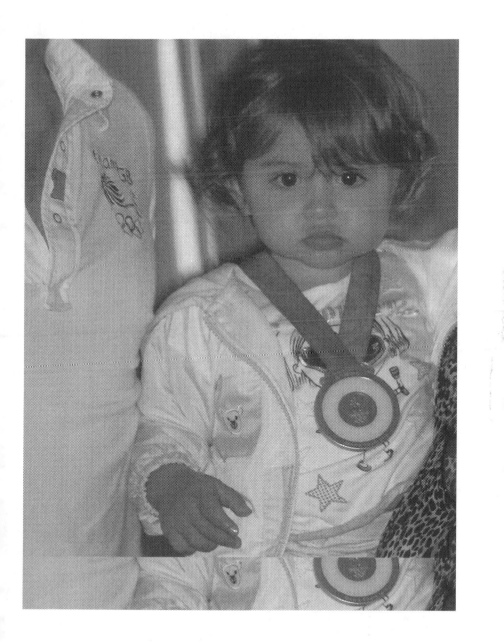